Get the Job

Fifty commonly asked
interview questions
and answers

Rebecca D. Matiku

Rebecca D. Matiku

Get the Job: Fifty commonly asked interview questions and answers

Copyright © 2015 Rebecca D. Matiku

This edition is a self publication

Rebecca D. Matiku
PO BOX 33984
Dar es Salaam, Tanzania
Printed in Tanzania

ISBN: 978 9976 89 442 4

All rights reserved. No part of this book may be used or reproduced in any manner whatsoever without written permission of the author, except in the case of brief quotations in articles and reviews.

Printed by Abana Printers Ltd.
PO BOX 23442
Dar es Salaam, Tanzania
Email: abanalimited@gmail.com

Dedication

To my father, BRIG. GENERAL Daniel Timothy Matiku (*rtd*)
and my mother, Deborah Marwa Kerambo

Contents

Chapter 1: Introduction 1

Chapter 2: What is an Interview? 12

Chapter 3: Methods of Interviewing 15

Chapter 4: 50 commonly asked interview questions and answers 19

Conclusion 44

References 45

CHAPTER 1

Introduction

Almost everyone in life, at least once will have the opportunity to go for a job interview. It is the most important part for you to win a job as it is when you get a chance to meet your future employer. Apart from having a good résumé which may make you noticed, having a chance to market yourself in person may have a great influence in landing you a job.

Rehearsing your answers and researching about the perspective of the employer is a great step to sharpen your job interview skills. It is also important to make a good first impression through how you dress, how you speak, and what you do.

This book focuses on four key issues that an interviewee should be aware of before participating in an interview. First, it talks about the job search skills and strategies, second, the different types of approaches of interviews and how you can get prepared for each of them. Third, the types of interviewers and how you can handle them.

Fourth, it has given the fifty most commonly questions asked in interviews and how to answer them. The answers have important details that the interviewee should take note of and also some sample answers for some questions have been given.

The ultimate aim of this book is to equip future employees through their job search journey. By taking advantage of the ideas offered here, you are assured to be successful in your next job interview and every other after that.

Job search skills and strategies

Have you ever asked yourself why someone less qualified than you got hired instead of you? Well, the answer is simple – it is the candidate with the best job search skills and strategies who gets hired.

The following are some of the skills that one should apply while searching for a job.

1) Self assessment

Self-assessment is the first step graduates should consider before starting the process of job searching. In the exercise of assessing yourself, note down what you mostly enjoy doing. Identify what it is you want to offer and what gives you job satisfaction. Other things to consider include what you do best and what's important to you.

Assessing yourself will give you direction towards the job search process and prepare you for the most common interview questions.

Note: Always remember to identify the skills you developed through your academic and co-curricular experience.

2) Set your goals

Now that you have assessed yourself and identified the skills you want to offer, the next step is setting goals. The best way to approach this step is to find out what job options appeal to you then put your focus on the few which match what you've learned about yourself.

3) Prepare an effective résumé

A résumé is a short document describing your personal information i.e. name, date of birth, telephone number, address *etc.* education and work history. It is given to an employer when you are applying for a job. Most employers spend 30–45 seconds checking applicants' résumés. It is advisable that your résumé be attractive, effective and above all quickly and easily digested.

It is obvious that not everyone has the same education or work history. This explains why there are different types of résumés. There are three main ones, which are; chronological résumé, functional résumé and combination résumé.

a) Chronological résumé

This type of résumé begins by listing your work history. You should start with your most recent position first and continue in reverse chronological order. With each position listed make sure you have mentioned the key accomplishments and qualifications so as to give the potential employer an idea of what kind of work you did and what they should expect from you. What follows is an education section which lists the schools you have attended and when, the degree(s) acquired, your major(s) and minor(s) and any other certificates or diplomas. If you have also acquired any honors or awards you should list them.

Fresh graduates who have no work experience should list their education history first then followed by their skills. Additional information like computer skills, laboratory skills, languages spoken among others are an added advantage.

A chronological résumé is the most preferred résumé because it eases up the employer's work of scanning which jobs you have done, when you did them and what you accomplished. This type of a résumé is of great advantage to those with a good work history.

Below is a sample of a chrnological résumé.

Sample Chronological Résumé for a Retail Position

Fredrich Kiribo
6 Pine Street
Arlington, VA 12333
555.555.5555 (home)
566.486.2222 (cell)
email:phjones@vacapp.com

Experience
***Key Holder*, Montblanc**
April 2009 – Present

- Opened new specialty boutique
- Place orders to restock merchandise and handled receiving of products
- Manage payroll, scheduling, reports, email, inventory, and maintain clientele book and records
- Integrated new register functions
- Extensive work with visual standards and merchandising high-ticket items

***Sales Associate*, Nordstrom - Collectors and Couture Departments**

July 2007 – April 2009

- Merchandised designer women's wear
- Set-up trunk shows and attended clinics for new incoming fashion lines
- Worked with tailors and seamstresses for fittings
- Scheduled private shopping appointments with high-end customers

***Bartender*, Jigg's Corner**
February 2005 – July 2007

- Provided customer service in fast-paced bar atmosphere

- Maintained and restocked inventory
- Administrative responsibilities included processing hour and tip information for payroll and closing register

Education
Bachelor of Arts, **Ramapo College, Arlington, VA**

Computer Skills
- Experienced in social media and Internet research

b) Functional Résumé

In this type of résumé, the focus is mainly on the skills acquired rather than the positions one has held. A few key areas of experience are usually highlighted and list responsibilities and accomplishments for each area of experience. The skill cluster should target the jobs you are applying for.

A functional Résumé is most preferable for fresh graduates with no work experience, or for those whose work history has breaks in service, for example, if you took time out to go to school or to raise children. This type of résumé can also benefit job seekers who want to change their careers to a field different from their previous experience.

However, keep in mind that functional résumés are not preferred by many employers. The following is an example of fuctional résumé.

Sample Functional Résumé – Management

Jose A. Adelo
1525 Jackson Street, City, NY 11111
Phone: 555-555-5555
Email: jadelo@bac.net

Objective

To obtain a position where I can maximize my multilayer of management skills, quality assurance, program development, training experience, customer service and a successful track record in the blood banking care environment.

Summary of qualifications

Results-oriented, high-energy, hands-on professional, with a successful record of accomplishments in the blood banking, training and communication transmission industries. Experienced in phlebotomy, blood banking industry, training, quality assurance and customer service with focus on providing the recipient with the highest quality blood product, fully compliant with FDA cGMP, Code of Federal Regulations, AABB accreditation and California state laws.

Major strengths include strong leadership skills, excellent communication skills, competent, strong team player, attention to detail, dutiful respect for compliance in all regulated environments and supervisory skills including hiring, termination, scheduling, training, payroll and other administrative tasks. Thorough knowledge of current manufacturing practices and a clear vision to accomplish the company goals. Computer and Internet literate.

Professional accomplishments
Program/Project Manager

- Facilitated educational projects successfully over the past two years for Northern California blood centers, a FDA regulated manufacturing environment, as pertaining to cGMP, CFR's, CA state and American Association of Blood Bank (AABB) regulations and assure compliance with 22 organization quality systems.

- Provided daily operational review/quality control of education accountability as it relates to imposed government regulatory requirements in a medical environment.

- Assisted other team members in veni-punctures, donor reaction care and providing licensed staffing an extension in their duties by managing the blood services regulations documentation (BSD's) while assigned to the self-contained blood mobile unit (SCU).

- Successfully supervised contract support for six AT&T Broadband systems located in the Bay Area. Provided customer intervention/resolution, training in telephony and customer care, Manpower

Scheduling, Quality Control, Payroll and special projects/plant extensions and evaluations to ensure proper end-of-line and demarcation signal.
- Reduced employee turnovers, introduced two-way communication to field employees, enhanced employee appearance and spearheaded the implementation of employee (health) benefits.
- Chief point of contact for the AT&T telephone and the ABC Affiliated TV stations as it relates to complaints and diagnosing communicational problems either at the site or remote broadcasting. Also tested/repaired prototype equipment for possible consideration or for future use.
- Reviewed FAA safety requirements and procedures to ensure compliance for aircraft and passenger safety.
- Communication expert and programming specialist for the intermediate range Lance and Persian missile systems. Trained to operate and repair the (FDC) fire direction control computer system and field satellite communications.
- Supervised and maintained the position of System Technician in charge of status monitoring and the integration of monitoring devices in nodes and power supplies. For the reception and transmission of telemetry to the network operation centers (NOC's) located in Denver, CO and Fremont, CA. Designed plant extensions, improved the paper flow and inventory control for the warehouse. Provided preventative maintenance at the system level, face to face customer interaction when required and traveled to several telephony/@home systems in the U.S. for evaluation and suggestions in using the status monitoring equipment.

Education
- Associate of Art, Administration of Justice, San Jose University, San Jose, CA
- NCTI Certified, CATV System Technician, Denver, CO
- ABM Certified, Cornerstone Technician, Denver, CO

c) Combination résumé or chrono-functional résumé

This type of résumé allows you to choose from both the chronological and functional types depending on your most relevant information. For a fresh graduate, history of education is more important than the last job, while for an experienced worker the years of professional work and experience gained are more important than education history.

The following is an example of a combination résumé.

Shirley Adams
1234 56 th Avenue
Apartment #203
Tucson, AZ 85725
(520) 555-5555

Summary
Dependable General Office Worker with more than 10 years of transferable experience. Proven clerical, customer service, and communication skills in a variety of settings. Upbeat, positive attitude with a history of producing quality results and satisfied customers. Computer literate.

Selected skills
General Office
- Organized and implemented group activities in an efficient manner
- Scheduled appointments and assured timely arrival
- Maintained accurate financial records, and paid all invoices on time
- Answered phones and took accurate messages
- Prepared reports and created documents using MS Word and WordPerfect
- Located desired information using the Internet

Customer Service
- Welcomed customers and visitors in a friendly and courteous manner
- Provided customers/clients with desired information in a timely manner

- Listened, calmed, and assisted customers with concerns
- Established friendly and lasting relationships

Communication
- Utilized Internet email as an effective communication tool
- Answered phones in a courteous and professional manner
- Established rapport with diverse individuals and groups
- Demonstrated ability to express ideas in a team environment and influence action

Related volunteer experience

General Office Volunteer - Salvation Army – Tucson, AZ – 5 Years
Event Coordinator- Neighborhood Involvement Program – Phoenix, AZ–3 Years
Group/Activities Leader - Girl Scouts of America – Phoenix, AZ – 4 Years
Family Manager - Self-employed – Tucson, AZ – 7 Years

Education
GED: Maricopa County Action Program, Phoenix, AZ

Apart from a résumé or curriculum vitae there is another document called a **cover letter**.

A cover letter is a letter of introduction attached to, or accompanying another document such as a résumé. Job seekers usually send cover letters along with the résumé as a way of introducing themselves to the employers and explaining their interest in the job. Employers easily use the cover letters to screen out applicants who lack the necessary basic skills.

4) Establish a powerful network

Networking is a very important and effective strategy in job searching. Connections are useful in accessing career advice, getting information about interviews, and getting the general support through the job searching process. Some students are lucky to get recruited while in campus and many others secure their first jobs through connections with friends and family friends, college alumni, previous internships and job supervisors, and faculty. Always remember that these contacts are just volunteering to help you. Therefore, you should not take them for granted or act as if you are entitled to their help.

Before meeting or having a phone conversation with the person helping you find a job, you are supposed to send a résumé and letter in advance. In your interaction you should reflect a clear focus by asking articulate questions, a precise request for advice, job leads and names or information of other experts in their networks that can assist you. After the interaction you should always send a thank you letter and a phone call to keep your network contact updated with the progress you have made.

Note: *In the interaction always be persistent in getting network leads.*

5) Apply for position

Before starting the process of job application, one is required to find a list of job offers from various sources. Some colleges have career centers which offer on-campus recruitment programs and job listings. Other sources are newspaper adverisements and your network contacts are also likely to produce some leads.

Make preparations of a good cover letter that can easily market your skills and experiences. Most importantly, highlight specific aspects of your education, work or co-curricular activities that are relevant to the job position.

It is wise to keep copies of all of your job correspondence. Follow up each job application with a telephone call to confirm if they have received your résumé and cover letter and also to get information about the possibilities of a job interview. When making the telephone calls always be polite and professional. Do not appear to be very demanding and overbearing.

6) Prepare for the job interview

After having the assurance of an interview, the ball rolls back to you. You now have homework of researching about the organization which has invited you for an interview. There are many sources of information that you can use, for example, a library, talking to people in your network, reading journals and magazines, the internet, among others.

You should also be aware of your skills in tackling interviews. There are various ways one can improve their skills, e.g. by reading interview guides and books and also by attending interview workshops.

Come up with questions and formulate possible answers. You can practice with a friend so that you can identify your mistakes. This book has fifty job interview questions and answers which are discussed in Chapter Four. Make use of them by practicing.

In your preparations you should be able to come up with questions that you will ask the interviewer after the interview. Finally, show the interviewer that you are sincerely interested in the job, that you will be delighted to work in their organization.

7) Gauge offers

At this stage the main focus is on your chances of your survival in the job. Look at the environment. Is it conducive enough for you to do your best? Can the positions offer you professional growth? If it is your first job, does it offer a firm foundation for your career? When it comes to evaluating the salary offers be realistic as you are the one in better position to know what suits you.

Rebecca D. Matiku

CHAPTER 2

What is an Interview?

The word interview has its origin from Latin and middle French words meaning to 'see each other' or to 'see between'.

An **interview** is a two-way communication between an interviewer and interviewee. Questions are usually asked mainly to enable the interviewer get explicit facts or details from the interviewee.

The person who asks questions in an interview is called an **interviewer** while the one responding to the questions is called an **interviewee.**

Types of interviewers

There are different types of interviewers just like there are different types of interviewees. Personality and the interview style play a big role on what the outcome of an interview will be. Familiarizing yourself with the different types of interviewers is a good strategy to enable you to deal with each of them. The following are the types of interviewers and how to handle them.

1) The interrogator

The interrogator is a type of an interviewer who asks questions throughout the interview. They are not interested in conversations. Do not expect any information from them to help you assess your performance. They just come to the interview room with a list of questions ready to fire off.

The best way to handle this kind of an interviewer is to stay calm, focus on answering the questions to the best of your knowledge and do not be scared by the interviewer's reactions. Throughout the interview you may feel defensive and probably after the interview you may feel like you did something wrong. As long as you gave the right answers then you have nothing to worry about on your part, it is just the interviewer's behaviour that is giving you such feelings.

2) The friendly interviewer

This kind of an interviewer has too much of everything. On welcoming you they will have a wide smile, enthusiastic handshake and above all the conversation will be too personal. You might be confused on how to act, because on one hand you might feel it's okay to relax but on the other hand you remember it's an interview.

The best way out with this kind of an interviewer is to be flexible. Do not be rigid in the interview as the prospective employer does not want an uptight employee. It is okay to show the interviewer that you are relaxed but don't forget to stay professional because you are the one being interviewed no matter how friendly the interviewer is. Do not engage in stories of wild parties and personal life – they do not belong here.

3) The one who is occupied by other things

Here the interviewer will be busy checking her phone, emails and other messages. They don't pay attention to you or what you say. With this kind of interviewer, do not take it personal as some of them may have been forced to participate in the interview process or they simply don't have the interest. Being friendly and holding the conversation might help win her/him over.

4) *The "by the rule" interviewer*

This type is not as harsh as the interrogator. They only try to abide to the rules and the pre existing interview script. They can't dare to go outside the everyday business interviewing protocol.

Get the Job

CHAPTER 3

Methods of Interviewing

a) Live interviews (in-person)

This is the most common method that has been used over time. Mostly it is a team of two and more interviewers per interviewee. Your non verbal and verbal communication should be articulated to reflect positivity.

If you are being interviewed by more than one person make sure you focus on the person asking the question so that you fully understand the question.

b) Telephone Interview

Most people are used to one on one interview and they have no idea that different companies have different ways of interviewing their prospective employees. Some employers use telephone interviews as a way of identifying and screening candidates in order to narrow the number of applicants who will be invited for the in-person interviews. It is an approach that reduces the expenses involved in interviewing out-of-town candidates.

When you apply for a job you should always be prepared for a phone interview because you never know when an employer or a networking contact will give you a call and ask if you can spare a few minutes to talk.

Prepare yourself for a phone interview just like you would for a an in-person interview. You can do this in the following ways:

- Look for a quiet, comfortable and private space. If you are at home, make sure the kids, spouses, significant others and pets are not around you. Close the door.
- Have your résumé on your fingertips, keep it in a clear view so that it is easy to look at and respond to questions.
- Compile a list of your strengths and weaknesses, qualifications and skills as well as answers to other typical phone interview questions.
- Have a pen and a paper at hand for note taking.
- Have a list of your accomplishments ready for review.
- Make sure that you are using the proper phone interview etiquette by answering the phone by yourself. When you answer the phone, say your name e.g. Deborah Nathaniel so that the interviewer knows they are talking to the right person.
- When the interviewer introduces himself/herself at the beginning of the interview, it is important for you to note/remember the name so that during the interview/conversation you can use his/her specific name. Mr or Ms and their last name.Only use their first name if they ask you to. Otherwise, use the formal title.
- Be more of a listener by not interrupting. If you have a question or you want to say something, jot it down on your paper and mention it when it's your turn to talk.

- Don't be silent for too long if you need a few seconds to gather your thoughts. Also if you need the interviewer to repeat a question, ask.
- You should have good telephone communication skills, i.e. during the phone interview you are supposed to sound as professional as you would if you were meeting the interviewer in-person.
- Don't chew gum or eat while you're on the phone.
- Smiling helps in an interview as it makes the tone of your voice more pleasant.
- Speak slowly, clearly and give simple explanations to questions so that the interviewer can continue asking more questions.

Remember to ask for the interviewer's email address and send out an email thank you note immediately, thanking the interviewer and emphasizing your interest in the job. You can also ask what the next step will be.

c)   **Videoconferencing or Skype Interview**

Videoconferencing

It is defined as the holding of a conference among people at remote locations by means of transmitted audio and video signals.

Skype

Skype is software application and online service that enables voice and video phone calls over the Internet. To skype is to make voice or video calls over the internet using the skpe app.

Video interviews are becoming common in the work place. This is because hiring has become global (Internet recruiting) for both employers and candidates. You should always remember that a video interview carries the same weight as the in-person interview. Therefore, this calls for preparation before the process.

You should do the following:
- Advance planning, which includes sending the résumé which is needed by the recruiter in advance. Arrive early if the interview will be done in the company so as to get oriented. You should ask for assistance if the technology is too advanced for your use.
- You should be properly dressed just like you would for an in-person interview.
- You should be careful not to make noise with your papers and pen since the microphone picks up all noises in the interview room. Eye contact is important.
- The interview questions will be the same like for the in-person interview, so you should be prepared.

d) Taped interview

This kind of interview is rarely used. Companies interviewing a big number of people for the same position prefer this method. It saves them time in reviewing candidates' answers since all the questions might be the same.

What to do when you go for this kind of an interview:
- More focus should be kept on the question because you will not be able to clarify it.
- Before proceeding you should review the instructions carefully because taped interviews are always timed.

Chapter 4

50 most commonly asked Interview questions and answers

The following are the commonly asked interview questions and how to answer them.

1. Tell me a bit about yourself:

This is the most frequently asked question in interviews. Having a short statement prepared in your mind is a great step to answering this question without having to look for what to say during the interview. You should be able to sound yourself. Focus on work-related issues unless instructed otherwise. You should consider talking about professional tasks you have done and job experiences you have had starting with the oldest and finilizing with the current one that relates to the position you are being interviewed for. For example, list five strengths that are related to the job, which can include experiences, traits and skills.

Rebecca D. Matiku

Sample answer

"I have been in the customer service industry for the past three years. My recent experience has been handling incoming calls in a telecommunication company (you can mention the company's name). I enjoy this particular job despite its challenges mainly because I get an opportunity to connect with people. In my last job I formed very good customer relationships resulting in a 40 percent increase in sales in a matter of two months".

Don't put yourself as a third party when you are talking about yourself e.g. "John is strong in communication, connecting with people, and has a reputation of meeting deadlines." Rather say, you are strong in communication, connecting with people and you have a reputation of meeting deadlines.

Conclude with a statement about your current aspiration. "What I am looking for now is a company that values customer relations, where it will be easy for me to join a strong, efficient and effective team so as to have a positive impact on customer retention and sales."

2. Why did you leave your previous job?

When answering this question stay positive regardless of the circumstances. Never refer to a major problem with management and never speak ill of supervisors, co-workers or the organization. If you do, you will be the one looking bad and there is a great chance of them distrusting you. Don't show your emotions to the question by changing your sitting position or postures. Rather, be neutral and keep smiling. Talk about leaving for a positive reason such as a new opportunity, a chance to do something special or other forward-looking reasons.

Here are some of the answers you can give to this question:
- To be honest, the position I was working in did not fit my career path so I found it reasonable to resign from the job and refocus on my career goals.

- I've been working as a temporary staff, so I left that job because I am looking for a permanent position.
- I left my previous job because there were limited opportunities for advancements and I wanted to further my career.
- I resigned due to family circumstances, but now I am settled and flexible to adapt to the working conditions of a full-time job.

If you did not leave the job voluntarily but instead was fired and an interviewer asks if you were fired, the following answers are the best.

- My competencies and skills were not the right match for my former employer's need when the company restructured, but I am sure that they will be a perfect fit for your organization.
- Although circumstances forced me to leave my previous job, I was very successful in school and I had good relations with both students and staff. Perhaps I neither understood what my bosses' expectations were from me nor why he had to release me so quickly before I had a chance to prove myself.

Practice in advance what you will say. Keep it brief, honest and moving so that you get to talk about your skills and why you think you qualify.

3. Do you consider yourself successful?

This question enables the recruiter to determine how you performed in previous positions. You should always answer positively, that you consider yourself a success and briefly explain why. A good explanation is that you have set goals, and you have met some and are on track to achieve the others. When answering this question make sure you look the recruiter in the eye and sell the statement with confidence.

You should have a copy of your résumé on hand, so that you can refer to each position by naming the accomplishments, the challenges you went through, and the skills you used to bring out positive results.

Sample answer

Yes, I do consider myself successful as I always give my best to my clients and all my tasks. I was rewarded with a promotion from a course advisor to assistant lecturer in my previous job. However, I'm not settled on that I intend to work harder so that I grow in what I do to become the best.

Or you could say:

I consider myself successful. My ability of taking new challenges makes me successful because I am flexible, I learn new things quickly, and I swiftly adapt to new tasks. You can give an example of an incident when you had to deal with a challenging task.

If you have no work experience, here is how to answer this question.

I consider myself successful because of my friendly personality, I get along with others. When I was in university/school/college I volunteered in various school activities because I have good communication skills. I was awarded several trophies and certificates of appreciation for my hard work.

4. What do co-workers say about you?

The reason why this question is asked during interviews is to enable the interviewer assess your relationship with co-workers and your role in a team. Also the recruiter would want to know if you are a person who is flexible enough to cope with the existing team dynamics, someone who can pick up other people's slacks when they are not working, and a person who can solve conflicts and not cause them.

When answering what the co-workers say about you don't forget to quote one or two statements from co-workers. Either a specific statement or a paraphrase will work. For example, "Jane Smith, a co-worker at Africa Advertisements Company, always said I was the hardest worker she had ever known." It is as powerful as Jane having said it at the interview herself.

If you are a fresh graduate with no work experience, the best way to answer this question is by referring to what your group members in school used to say about you.

5. What experience do you have in this field?

Speak about specifics that relate to the position you are applying for. If you do not have specific experience, get as close as you can. You don't want to partially market yourself in an interview with this question. This question offers you time to tell the interviewer about any experiences that you might have that are relevant to the position and makes you the perfect candidate for the job. You have to be specific by talking about the school, previous jobs that you may have done, or any prior life experiences that have molded you for the position.

Quote:

"We do not hire experts neither do we hire men on past experiences or for any position other than the lowest. Since we do not take a man on his past history, we do not refuse him because of his past history. I never met a man who was thoroughly bad. There is always some good in him if he gets a chance."

Henry Ford

6. What do you know about this company?

This question is one reason why you should do some research on the organization before the interview. Find out where they have been and where they are going. If you are a college graduate you can approach the career office in your school so as to get a list of alumni who work for the company. This will enable you get an insider's view of the job and also get information that is not available elsewhere.

Another method is by checking the company's website so as to review the information offered by the employer. Social media like the company's Facebook page, and Twitter handle are also a good platform for you to check out so as to see what information the company is sharing and promoting. This can enable you to get hints of information that you may use during the interview.

You can go an extra mile by researching on the people who will interview you. Review their LinkedIn profiles and Google them to see if you can get any information. The more you discover about them the more comfortable you will be during the interview.

The research made about the company will assist you to make a good impression on how much you know about the company.

7. Are you applying for other jobs?

Be honest but do not spend a lot of time in this area. Keep the focus on the job you are being interviewed for and what you can do for that organization. Anything else is a distraction.

Sample answer
To be honest, yes I am. I have been searching for a job in a suitable organization that my skills, knowledge and experience would add value to its operations, and I have found it. It will be a great opportunity for me to work here and help the organization achieve its goals.

8. What have you done to improve your skills in the last year?

Try to include improvement activities that relate to the job. A wide variety of activities can be mentioned as positive self-improvement. The answer to this question should also match the résumé and cover letter. A tip on how to answer this question is natural curiosity, which has a direct effect on one's problem-solving skills. College courses, self-study, and any other goal-oriented not work related are good examples.

Sample answer
- When I experienced a difficult task I used to seek help from a friend or colleague who was promoted to the same job I am aiming for. I sat with them and keenly observed how they did their tasks. From that I practised and applied the techniques, some worked for me while others did not.
- I did a course that was useful for the next project. I also participated in seminars on career development and improvement of marketing skills (or any other relevant skills).

9. Why are you interested in working for this company?

This question is looking for a similar thing as, "Why are you interested in this company?" or "Why are you interested in the job?" This question may require some thought and certainly, should be based on the research you have done on the organization. Sincerity is extremely important here and will easily be sensed. The following are some of the guidelines you should consider when answering this question.

- Relate it to your long-term career goals and how it will fit into your plan.
- Find out what you know about the organization, industry and position.
- Understand your priorities and preferences – which aspects of the company and/or job are appealing to you and why.

You should be sincerely interested in the job and will perform effectively and efficiently if hired.

Another question close to this is, "What do you like about this company?" Here, the hiring manager is mainly looking for an employee who will fit in at the company and enjoy working there. Good answers to this will portray knowledge of the company. This means that you have to do research so as to identify precise reasons for the need of that position in the organization.

These reasons could include the following:
- General company reputation
- The quality of products/services
- Company values
- Reputation of key leaders
- How the company rewards its employees
- Company positioning in the market
- Company growth/success

Avoid giving the following answers to this question:

- An answer that is too general and could apply to any company, e.g. "It's a great company and I'd love to work here". It's a good answer but only that it's not memorable and believable.
- An unenthusiastic answer that makes the interviewer wonder if you really want the job, e.g. "I heard there were some open positions so I came."
- An uninformed answer that shows you have not done any background check on the company, i.e. being unaware of what the company is involved in.

10. What kind of salary do you need?

This is a big question as it is the one that determines how much the company will pay you. It's a nasty little game that you will probably lose if you answer it directly. So, do not answer it. Instead, say something like, "That's a tough question. Can you tell me the range for this position?" By asking this question you will be safe since the interviewer will be caught off-guard. Another answer can be, "It depends on the details of the job". Then give a wide range. The reason why you don't have to give the precise amount of salary you want to be paid is because you might ask for a lower amount that the position offers or you might ask for too much and so the employer will see you as greedy.

11. Are you a team player?

All jobs that you can find will require you to be a team player or have some team skills. There is always social interaction at the workplace and some times you will have to work with others. When answering this question you should be able to answer with a resounding 'YES' and back it up with an explanation on how you can work with a team. You must have ready examples.

Specifics that show you often perform for the good of the team rather than for yourself are good evidence of your team attitude. Do not brag, just say it in a matter-of-fact tone. This is a key point.

There are other employees who do not like working in a team because they believe people are different and therefore disagree on how they perform their duties. If you fall under this group of employees it is important that you do not apply for a position that requires that skill.

Sample Answer
- "I tend to do well in a team setting because I get along with others well, have a professional attitude, and understand what it takes to get the job done. I can delegate tasks, perform them, compromise and fulfill any task assigned to the team. In terms of job performance I am flexible. I can work independently as well as on a team depending on the task at hand."

Quote:
"Putting on the same jersey doesn't make you a team. You're still just a collection of individuals until you find a common goal."
Harry Sinden, Former coach & president of the Boston Bruins

12. Do you know anyone who works for us?

Be aware of the policy on relatives working for the organization. This can affect your answer even though they asked about friends, not relatives. This question is asked so that the interviewer can

know the following:
- If you are like the people she/he likes or the ones she/he does not like.
- If the relation you have with the person in that company will bring conflicts.
- If you will be able to separate your work from personal relationships.

Therefore, your answer should address these concerns and make the interviewer get a positive aspect that will make you the best fit for the job.

Sample answer
- "I know that Rebecca, will be a good mentor, and I'm sure she will give me good advice as I grow with the organization. More importantly I want you to know that I have made this decision on my own and I am ready to develop my own career with the company."

13. How long would you expect to work for us if hired?
It is not good to be too specific here. Answers like this should work:
- "I would like to work here for a long time ..." Or "As long as we both feel I'm doing a good job."
- "I don't have plans to move on in the near future. So I'd like a job where I can have continuity and be part of a team."

14. Have you ever been required to fire anyone? How did you feel about that?
This is serious. The interviewer mainly wants to know if you can keep the good of the company against personal loyalties or morals when making necessary actions within the organization. Do not make light of this question or appear to like firing people. At the same time, indicate that you will do it when it is the right thing to do. When it comes to the situation where you have to defend

the organization versus the individual who has created a harmful situation, say that you will protect the organization. Remember, firing is not the same as lay-offs or reduction in workforce. Also be honest if you have never fired an employee. In such a scenario the interviewer might ask you to consider what you will feel like if you fired someone.

Sample answer:

Considering the company's policies, principles and sequence on individual penalty procedures, those who were late at work portrayed bad behavior and those that couldn't fulfill their duties in a duly manner were frequently laid off. I didn't like these kinds of employees; however, I still excused them somehow.

One of the most difficult tasks as a manager is to fire someone. I think the best way to handle this problem is to be more reasonable and professional so that both parties feel relived and satisfied with the decision.

Quote:

"I was asked if I was going to fire an employee who made a mistake that cost the company $600,000. No, I replied. I just spent $600,000 training him. Why would I want somebody to hire his experience?"
Thomas John Watson, First CEO of IBM.

15. What is your philosophy towards work?

A question like this is mostly asked to managers, high level executives and team leaders. It is also asked to other professionals such as nurses, social workers and teachers. The interviewer is not looking for a long or flowery dissertation here. The answer that the interviewer will be expecting is the one that will reflect maturity, experience, enthusiasm, strong work ethics and keenness.

Do you have strong feelings that the job should get done? Type of answer that works best here should be short and positive, e.g. "Yes."

Another important thing you should remember here is that honesty should be adhered to. Most interviewees are not good liars while most interviewers are very good at spotting dishonesty. It will not bring a good image of you if you are caught being dishonest. Honesty and enthusiasm is what attracts employers and not an image of exaggerated perfection.

Some of the best work philosophies that one can consider are:
- Teamwork
- Focus
- A hundred percent effort
- Creativity
- Leadership
- Uniqueness
- Motivation
- Resourcefulness
- Helping/Serving
- Act of Balancing
- Vision
- Learning from mistakes

16. If you had enough money to retire now, would you?

This question needs an honest answer from you. If you feel like you will retire, be affirmative and if you feel like you won't, just decline. Again on the issue of enough money, it largely depends on what amount exactly because 20 million to the interviewer could be enough money but it might not be the same for the interviewee. But since you need to work, and you like the job being offered, do not say yes if you don't mean it.

17. Tell us how you would be an asset to this organization.

This question gives you an opportunity to summarize and highlight your best points and qualifications in relation to the position you are being interviewed for. The following are some of the assets you can talk about in the interview which you will offer the organization.

- Adaptable and manages change well
- Motivated and always determined
- Continous learner
- Accepts postivive critism
- A strong communicator
- Always appropriate and professional
- Reliable
- Keeps the big picture in mind, never loses focus
- Resourceful and investigative
- Values others' time, treats everyone with the same importance
- Self awareness

18. Why should we hire you?

Think of an equivalent question to this which could be, "Why should we buy your product?" It is clear that this question is all about marketing yourself. It is a question that can take you off the road when answering so you always have to think ahead so as to be on the safe road. The answer to this question can start with, "Because I am a good fit for the position." Then, point out how your assets meet what the organization needs. Never mention or compare yourself to any candidate.

19. Have you ever been asked to leave a position?

The best advice here is that you should not talk about the jobs you left and so they should not be part of your résumé. You do not want to have a list of companies you have been fired from in your CV. You can only talk about the company you left if it was because there was a better position offered or the company went bankrupt. Simply say no if you have never been fired and if you have, and feel like the reasons will not ruin your chances of getting employed then be honest, brief and avoid saying negative things about the people or organization involved.

20. Tell me about a suggestion you have ever offered that made a difference.

The answer to this question should reflect that you are enthusiastic, resourceful, positive to your work and proactive in your approaches. Be sure and use a suggestion that was accepted and became successful. By doing this the interviewer will identify interesting insights about you – that you can influence people in your approach.

21. What irritates you about co-workers?

The real deal with this question is that the interviewer is not interested in hearing the stories about other people but rather knowing how you deal with challenging behaviours or personalities of co-workers in the working environment. Simply put, this question is a trap and you should think real hard. Do not come up with anything that irritates you. At the end just say you seem to get along with colleagues. If you have encountered difficult personalities and you feel like talking about it, the number one rule should be staying professional when responding to this question and avoid being negative. Generalize about the colleagues and the situation.

22. Tell me about your dream job.

Stay away from a specific job, even if your dream job may have nothing to do with the job you are applying for. You cannot win. Try as much as possible to connect your answer with the job you are being interviewed for. The interviewer is mostly interested to know if you will be satisfied and motivated by the job on offer. The best way to say something like: "A job where I love the work, the people, and can freely contribute."

23. What makes you think you will do well in this job?

Answer the question from all angles by giving several reasons including your skills, experience, interests, and past successes which promote future successes.

24. What is your greatest strength?

This is one of the easiest questions you will be asked in the interview. The best answers to give should bring out the skills and experiences required for the position you have applied for. Giving numerous answers is a good approach but always stay positive.

Your answer can focus on:

- your ability to prioritize
- your problem-solving skills
- your ability to work under pressure
- your ability to focus on projects
- your professional expertise
- your leadership skills
- your positive attitude.

25. What are you looking for in a job?

This is the equivalent of, "Tell me about your dream job." See question number 22.

26. What kind of person would you refuse to work with?

Never admit a particular type of person unless it is known that the person is an obstacle to the company's growth and development. Don't dare to mention specific races, gender, classes, ethnic group, religion and political group when discussing this question. You can say that you like working under conditions that allow diversity as it is a platform for you to learn something from everyone so as to benefit the company.

27. What would your previous supervisor say your strongest strength is?

This question has a potential to reveal some important information about you. There are many good possibilities: Loyalty, Honesty, Energy, Positive attitude, Self-awareness, Leadership, Flexibility and adaptability, Team player, Reliable, Expert, taking initiative, Patience, Hard work, Creativity, Problem solver. For example, "I believe if you asked/talked to Daniel he would tell you that I was strong in building relations with customers. In fact there was a time I was assigned to deal with a difficult customer and at the end of the day we were able to have good relations with her too. This made me recognized in the company as my relationship building skills had a great contribution to both building trust and dealing with challenging situations appropriately."

28. Tell me about a problem you had with a supervisor.

This is the biggest trap of all. The item you need to include in your answer should show conflict resolution skills, good communication, and end with a good outcome. This is a test to see if you will speak ill of your former boss. Remember that if you focus on the negative side of your former supervisor you are the one who is going to give a bad image about yourself. Rather, stay positive and avoid talking about any problem with a supervisor.

29. What has ever disappointed you about a job?

Don't get negative. You should say, there wasn't enough of challenge, which would have given you a chance to improve your skills and have more responsibility, also when the company could have made more money but did not.

30. Tell me about your ability to work under pressure.

Give an example of a time when you achieved a desired outcome under obstacles such as time or budget. It should relate to the type of position applied for.

Sample answer
I have always been able to prioritize tasks so as to remain with a manageable workload.

31. What is more important to you: the money or the work?

As it is believed by many people, money is the most important. If we look at the other side of the coin, yes, money is important but there are jobs that you can not accept to do no matter the salary. This brings us to the point that work is the most important. There is no better answer. Also be careful as this question might be asked in different ways, at different times in the interview.

32. Do your skills match this job or are they more suitable for another closely related job?

This is a direct question asked so that the interviewer may know how you match the job qualifications. When answering, do not raise suspicions that you may want another job more than this one.

33. What motivates you to do the best while working?

This is a question that will reveal your inner psychology, experiences, and personality. They are items that only you can say. This could be challenges, achievements, recognition, affiliation and power. When answering, the interviewer will be able to find out whether you are a person who thinks of long-term goals or not.

34. Are you willing to work extra hours?

Here, say you are okay with extra hours and ready to put in a hundred percent into your work. However, this is entirely upon you. Be totally honest.

Sample answer:

It all depends on the responsibilities on your part, if my task will require me to work overnights and weekends I will gladly do it. I will be happy that I have completed my job on time.

Or you can say:

I can work in a few nights or weekends of overtime through the month if there are tight deadlines. I hope projects are schedule in a way that I will not be required to work overnight regularly.

35. How would you know you were successful in this job?

Don't confuse this question with an opportunity to brag. You are required to exercise self-awareness, motivation and analytical ability so as to answer this question appropriately. The recruiter is interested in knowing how successful you will be in the job, so it's best to back your facts with valid achievements.

36. Are you willing to put the interests of the organization before your own?

Simply be positive. Your answer should reflect loyalty and dedication. Do not bring the art of deep ethical and philosophical implications.

Sample answer:

The short and long term success of the company depends on my interest, so it is in my best interest to complete a task as the company requires of me.

If you feel uncomfortable with this question, you may ask for specific scenarios of when the question would become applicable. Common scenarios would be when you are asked to work extra hours especially when there are tight deadlines.

Note: Here the interviewer wants to know if the employee will meet the company's goals even at the expense of their personal time.

If your answer is NO, be honest and say it. Most employers prefer an employee who speaks their mind and gives an honest reason why they may not do as asked.

Sample answer:

No, my family comes first then my job.

37. Describe your management experience.

It can also be asked in another way, for example, "What is your management style?"

Generally, this question is asked to interviewees who are aspiring for managerial or executive positions. Do not label yourself e. g. progressive, salesman or consensus. Labeling yourself can have different meanings. To be safe, better say the situational style which is safe. If you say this, they will understand that you will manage according to the situation, instead of one size fits all.

38. Would you be willing to relocate or travel if required?

You should be honest. You don't have to say yes, yet you have no idea of how the job looks like in the first place. You might say yes and once you get employed you realize you do not like the job. As much as it depends on your personal decision, it is important to be clear on this with your family's prior to the interview if you think there is a chance it may come up.

You should be aware of the difference between relocation and traveling. Great advice is that you should always put into your consideration your family status and financial issues before answering this question.

39. What have you learned from mistakes on the job?

Give an answer with an example of something that was negative and turned into a positive lesson. An example would be working too far ahead of colleagues on a project and thus disrupting coordination. This made you realize that you can manage tasks individually and meet the deadline. However, do not mention a mistake that will ruin your chances of getting the job. Big companies like Microsoft, usually asks the interviewee the number of times he/she has failed in their life. If you say you have never failed then you do not qualify for a job. What they believe is that if you have never failed, then you have never learned anything new. Everyone makes mistakes, so it is okay to share your mistakes in an interview.

40. If you were hiring a person for this job, what would you look for?

Mention skills that are needed for the position and the ones you have. Keep your answer short and simple. Your résumé already convinced the interviewing panel you are qualified, that is why you were called for the interview. Do not spend a lot of time preaching about your qualifications unless you have been asked to do so.

Sample answer:

I would look for a candidate that has good communication skills, willing to help customers and does so in a pleasant manner. Also, I'd want a person who would grow sales through strong customer service skills and salesmanship. Drive is also a vital quality, I look for a candidate with the passion to break personal sales record.

If you were hiring a person for this job, what would you look for (in a new college graduate)?

You can also say:

I would look for a person with great communication skills, good mix of team work and leadership skills. A graduate with a strong blend of academic and industry experience. Lastly, an ambitious person who is also willing to learn from others within the company.

Quote

*"Somebody once said that in looking for people to hire, you look for three qualities:integrity,intelligence,a nd energy.And if you don't have the first, the other two will kill you. You think about it,it's true.If you hire somebody without (integrity),you really want them to be dumb and lazy." - **Warren Buffet.***

41. Do you think you are overqualified for this position?

This question should not intimidate a former manager interviewing for a low position in an organization. In fact if they ask you this question, it is obvious that they have gone through your résumé and they have seen that you highly qualify for the job. Regardless of your qualifications, you should always state that you are very well qualified for the position.

Don't downgrade yourself by trying to pretend that you are less than you actually are. Misrepresenting your experience and achievements will make you unsuccessful on selling yourself.

Sample answer:

I have worked at a higher level, but this position is exactly what I'm looking for. I have been searching for a job that is challenging but a little less intense so that I can create time to spend with my family.

42. Do you have any blind spots?

This question can also be asked in another way, "Do you have any weaknesses?"

Do not talk about failings. Failures are not blind spots. It is obvious that if you had blind spots, you would not know about them (meaning, if you know your blind spots, they are not blind spots any more). The question does not ask you to reveal your personal information either. Allow them to discover your blind points for themselves.

Rebecca D. Matiku

Sample answer:

None that I know of but I will be open to criticism if it helps me grow.

43. Propose how you will compensate for your lack of experience.

First, you should bring up your areas of experience that the interviewer is not aware of. Then, state that you are a hard worker, a quick learner and that you posses a strong workforce.

For a fresh graduate with no work experience this question may intimidate you but here is the good news, If they didn't think you were ready for the role, you wouldn't have gotten a call into the interview. Do not give them a chance to think that you are not the best candidate for the role by answering, "I will work hard and be the best employee the company has".

Sample answer:

Experience is only valuable if it helps you do a better job than someone without it. Yet I am confident I can handle the position's tasks competently, and I am willing to take all the training from mentors and team members seriously.

Quote:

"You only lack experience if they want it done the same old way."
Robert Brault

44. What qualities do you look for in a boss?

You should be optimistic, generic and positive. Some of the qualities can include, knowledge, honesty, a sense of humour, leadership, fairness, loyalty. All bosses think they have these traits.

Sample answer:

There are many qualities but the few that I can mention now are; A boss who can treat me with dignity, respect and equally. One that is honest and can have open communication with me. Above all, who can recognize me for my efforts and the value I provide to the company/organization.

45. What position do you prefer in a team working on a project?

Be honest. If you are not comfortable with some roles let them know, and also point out the areas that you are more comfortable to work in.

Sample answer:

To be frank, any position which I am capable of is my ideal position. I want to be in a position where I can fully utilize my skills and knowledge also blend with all my team members so as to come up with a successful project.

I want to work as a programmer (whatever position you are qualified in) in my team so as to use my skills and experience to deliver a quality work.

46. Describe your work ethics.

A person's work ethics reflects a person's feelings, attitude and beliefs about work responsibilities. It is those items that will determine how that person relates to occupational responsibilities. Such responsibilities include hard-work, reliability, goal-setting, task completion, accountability, honesty, cooperation, determination and leadership.

Sample answer:

My work ethic depend on values in the society, I put thought and consideration into what I do. I believe in immediate execution, delivering quality work and honesty. I take ownership in my job, I like what I do so it isn't ever 'just a job' for me.

47. Tell me about a time when you helped resolve a dispute between others.

Use a specific example. Do not talk about the conflict details, rather focus on your problem solving techniques.

Sample answer:

At my previous job, I once resolved a conflict between two members who could no longer work together. Their relationship not only affected our productivity but also the team. I separated the two and calmed them down. I then got in control to discuss the problem with both of them in a calm manner. I highlighted to them that a compromise must be reached so I tried to understand the perspectives of both parties without siding with either one. It was a challenge listening to their perspectives as both of them presented their arguments with no consideration of the other's perspective. To end this, I made them understand the need of having changes since the status quo was unworkable. We later agreed to amicable solutions, and emphasized that future disagreements should be handled professionally and should avoid getting emotional. After that there was a more pleasant work atmosphere.

48. What has been your biggest professional disappointment?

It is normal to get disappointments so be free to talk about it. You should refer to something that was beyond your control. Show acceptance and no negative feelings.

Sample answer:

I once tried to formulate an intricate sales proposal in half the time we normally allocated, because the client was in a rush. I failed to finish it in time, that was a big disappointment to me. The client did us a favor, she accepted the proposal though a few days after the deadline. It was a success because we wound up getting that order. As much as it was a disappointment at first, I learnt the importance of effective planning and communication.

49. Tell me about the most fun you have had while working.

This question can be asked in another way e.g. "Which job have you enjoyed the most?" The employer is interested in knowing what you like about working. Talk about having fun by accomplishing something for the organization.

Sample answer:

I did a project with co-workers which involved meeting new people, I enjoyed that task because, being a people person, I like collaborative work and it gave me an opportunity to make new friends.

I always celebrate when I meet or exceed goals because the accomplishments usually teach me something new.

50. Do you have any questions for us/me?

You might have up to ten questions but do not ask all of them. Choose two or three that are very important. Examples of questions to ask are as follows:

- What would be a typical work day/week be?
- Are there any advancement opportunities for an employee in this position?
- How soon will I be able to be productive?

Conclusion

Having discussed the Job Search skills and strategies, the types of Interviewers, Methods of Interviewing and the 50 commonly asked Interview questions and answers, this book will help you to:

- Prepare yourself for an interview.
- Advance your communication skills.
- Answer the most difficult questions.
- Handle different types of interviewers and interviewing methods.
- Avoid making mistakes during an interview.
- Identify what the interviewer wants to know from you with each question.

References

Mary Schilling (February 1997). Maths Horizon, How to find a Job. (pp.11-13) Vol.4, No.3

http://www.careerprofiles.info

http://www.everydayinterviewtips.com

http://www.freeinterviewquestions.info

http://www.4hrm.info

http://www.jobsearch.about.com

http://www.job-application.com

http://www.resumark.com

http://www.resumeworld.ca

Rebecca D. Matiku

About the author

Rebecca Matiku has studied International Relations. Her specialization is Diplomacy and Foreign policy, while her minor is Development Studies. She is an entrepreneur and a leader who has had great contributions at the United Nations where she participated in a panel discussion on challenges and opportunities for Security Sector Reform (SSR) in East Africa and the Horn of Africa organized by the Embassy/permanent mission of the Slovak Republic in Nairobi, UNON, UNIC, The Government of Republic of Kenya and IPSTC. She also participated in the Harvard National Model United Nations (HNMUN), 2015. She has been involved in charity work by serving the community in Nairobi, Kenya where she used to teach at Rescue Dada Rehabilitation Centre.

She attributes her authorship of *Get the Job* to the experiences she has had from the different countries she has been to, which include United States of America, Netherlands, Germany, Italy, France, Austria, Switzerland, United Arab Emirates (UAE), Egypt, Kenya and Tanzania, her home country.

For more information:
Call: + 255 763513347
          + 255 673878042
          + 254 707896961
Email: *getajobbyr1@gmail.com*
Facebook page: **Get the Job**

www.ingramcontent.com/pod-product-compliance
Lightning Source LLC
Chambersburg PA
CBHW071231160426
43196CB00012B/2483